Fire Chief Cars
1900-1997
Photo Album

By Donald F. Wood and
W. Wayne Sorensen

Iconografix
Photo Album Series

Iconografix Inc. exists to preserve history through the publication of notable photographic archives and the list of titles under the Iconografix imprint is constantly growing. Transportation enthusiasts should be on the Iconografix mailing list and are invited to write and ask for a catalog, free of charge.

Authors and editors in the field of transportation history are invited to contact the Editorial Department at Iconografix, Inc., PO Box 446, Hudson WI 54016. We require a minimum of 120 photographs per subject. We prefer subjects narrow in focus, e.g., a specific model, railroad, or racing venue. Photographs must be of high-quality, suited to large format reproduction.

Iconografix
PO Box 446
Hudson, Wisconsin 54016 USA

Iconografix books are offered at a discount when sold in quantity for
promotional use. Businesses or organizations seeking details should
write to the Marketing Department, Iconografix, at the above address.

Library of Congress Card Number: 98-71287

ISBN 1-882256-87-5

98 99 00 01 02 03 04 5 4 3 2 1

A chief's buggy in front of San Francisco's Station 25, just after the turn of the century. The driver is seated closest to us. Note the bell behind the seat and the gas street light behind the buggy.

INTRODUCTION

Modern fire apparatus is fast, powerful, and efficient. Carried on this apparatus are many tools dating from the past—such as hooks and ladders—along with those that have come into use in recent years—such as breathing gear and electric saws. Since the Civil War, when steam fire engines replaced the hand pumps, firefighting and firefighting equipment have kept pace with the rapid advances in firefighting science and engineering.

Anyone watching fire engines responding to a 911 call with sirens screaming and air horns blasting is likely to see another vehicle along with the apparatus—a chief's car, usually painted red, or red and white, with its own siren and flashing red lights. At the site of a fire the chief can be seen in white turn-out gear directing the firefighting operations.

The lineage of most of today's apparatus can be traced to horse-drawn rigs used a century ago. Thus some departments with long traditions still refer to the chief's auto as the "chief's buggy."

In large departments the chief of the department has a driver, but in smaller departments the chief must drive himself. In the early days of motor vehicles "civilian" chauffeurs drove the chief's car; later uniformed firefighters were the drivers.

The ranking uniformed officer in a department is the chief. In some departments the title of the chief is, in fact "chief engineer." This is because firefighting is sometimes referred to as a branch of engineering or science, taught at the college level. In most cities there is one chief officer and one or more deputy chiefs, as well as battalion chiefs and assistant chiefs. Large city fire departments are divided geographically into battalions consisting of three to five stations, under the command of a single battalion chief. In a department with several levels of chiefs, the ranking chief often has a higher-priced auto assigned to him.

Who is the chief? Most chief officers started at the bottom of their respective departments as firefighters. After written and oral examinations, a firefighter might be promoted to engineer, then to the rank of lieutenant or captain (a captain is in charge of an apparatus). Above the rank of captain are several levels of chiefs, and the top uniformed officer is the chief of the department.

Ordinarily, the chief of the department is selected from the roster of the department's ranking officers by the mayor or Police and Fire Commission. Although, sometimes a chief is appointed from another community. The chief of the department can select his deputy and other chiefs from the roster of officers who have already earned the rank of captain or higher.

What are the chief's duties? At the fire site the chief is the ranking officer and all other firefighters work under his command. Paid departments are paramilitary in structure. The chief has to work through this structure as he leads the department. The chief has to maintain the morale and discipline of all firefighters in his department.

Since firefighters in most large cities are unionized, one of the chief's challenges is to lead his firefighters in an organization that is both paramilitary and unionized. Firefighters are continually being trained, another key responsibility of the chief.

As head of a municipal department the chief often has to work with operating budgets that cover day to day expenses, plus a capital budget that provides funds for new stations and new equipment. He has to compete with other municipal department heads for funds, while working with the mayor, city manager, and city council. Because insurance underwriters' groups rate each community's firefighting capability, the chief is continually concerned with meeting their fire department criteria to insure fire insurance premiums in the community are kept low.

What is a chief's car? Most are conventional automobiles, although station wagons, light trucks, vans, and sport-utility vehicles are also used. (There is an unverified story that in large cities, Packard would supply the chief's auto free because of the publicity value.)

Over the years the cars carried some extra equipment. Some had bells used for signaling, and almost all chiefs' cars had a siren and flashing or rotating red lights. Most chiefs' cars probably carried one or two types of fire extinguishers, a first aid kit, the chief's turn-out gear, and extra air bottles. Two- and three-way radios came into use in the late 1930s and chief's cars have carried them ever since. Early vacuum-tube radios would consume half of the trunk's space. Today, command "consoles" fit easily into the rear of the chief's auto or van and contain sophisticated communication equipment, computers, and file drawers for maps, building plans, water supply information, and hazardous material response instructions.

We think of the chief's car moving in response to fire alarms, but that is only one of its duties. The chief is also the administrative head of a city department and has to conduct business with other city departments, as well as with the public. In addition, the chief is expected to visit the department's training center and stations throughout the city on a fairly regular basis. He is involved in area-wide "disaster response" planning, and he develops "mutual aid" relationships with departments in neighboring cities.

Relatively few chiefs' cars have been saved and restored. After their initial assignment, they would typically be used elsewhere in the department, such as by members of the arson squad. In the pages that follow, we will see chiefs' cars in a representative collection of photos.

We will also see some fire department "command posts" that utilize bus or van bodies. Fires, especially wild land fires, can take days to quell; and other incidents such as building collapses or hazardous material spills require uniformed personnel to be on the scene for a series of shifts. The command center is also a communications post because today every firefighter can carry a small radio which allows the chief to have a better idea of the disaster's dimensions and how to best deploy personnel and equipment. For example, San Jose, California's Fire Department has a new Command Post Support Vehicle called "Command One." It will be dispatched to all third alarms, plus serious high-rise or wild land fires. San Jose sends a dispatcher to these major incidents, and it is the dispatcher's duty to deploy, set up, and mobilize this vehicle.

This book covers fire chiefs' cars throughout the 20th Century. The major changes have been in the vehicles themselves and in improved communications.

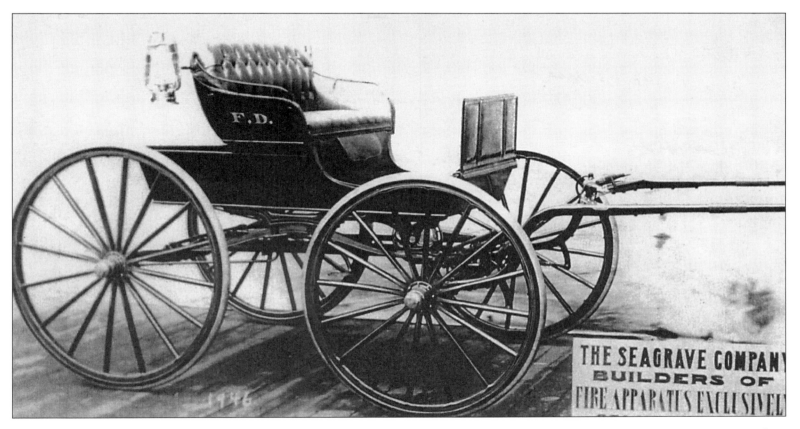

Seagrave (among the oldest existing fire apparatus builders in the U.S.) sold buggies for use by fire chiefs. Often the buggies were included with the purchase of larger apparatus.

New York City Fire Chief Croker at the tiller of a steam-powered 1901 Locomobile.

This 1903 Stanley steamer runabout was used to carry the fire chief in Newtonville, Ohio. Rig is steered by a tiller.

For a brief period of time, Mercedes autos were built in the U.S. This 1904 model (left) was used as a chief's car in New York City. Letters on radiator say: "FDNY."

A 1905 Worthington right-hand drive with both bell and siren. San Francisco's chief, Dennis T. Sullivan, is at right, and the driver is Ollie Hirst. Chief Sullivan was killed as the result of a building collapse during the 1906 San Francisco earthquake. Hirst later would build "Challenger" fire apparatus at a plant in Sacramento.

Fire Chief Frank Dowell, of Portland, Oregon, is on the right. The auto is a 1906 Ford Model N.

A circa-1906 Pope-Hartford used as an officer's car by the San Francisco Fire Department.

The chief's trumpet (right), through which he shouted orders, has long been the fire chief's symbol and sometime appears on insignia and uniform buttons. Often the number of trumpets on an officer's insignia signifies his rank. In 1906, the Waterous catalog offered both brass and nickel-plated versions, 16, 18, or 20 inches long, ranging in price from $3.50 to $7.00.

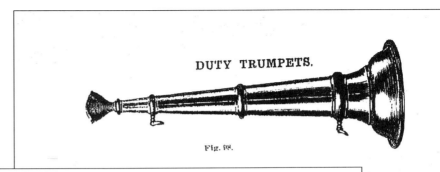

DUTY TRUMPETS.

Fig. 98.

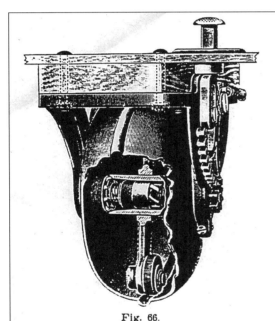

Fig. 66.

NEW DEPARTURE CHIEF'S BUGGY BELL.

Illustration showing interior mechanism. Finish—Full nickel plate throughout.

Price $25.00

This illustration is an end view with section of gong cut away, to show hammer and other operating mechanism. It will be noted that the moving parts are hung in double ball bearings, these bearings being of hardened steel, carefully fitted. The hammers are placed on opposite sides of the hammer arm, so that (as two gongs are here used) each hammer strikes its respective gong. The two gongs are so calculated and tuned that a chime is produced, of exceeding strength and penetration, and unlike any other bell ever used.

FIRE PROTECTION ALWAYS PAYS

Waterous (which still builds pumps) advertised this buggy gong in its 1906 catalog. It was placed under the floorboard and was rung by stepping on a button mounted above the floorboard.

Fire Department Headquarters, Newton Centre, Mass.

A circa-1906 Stanley Steamer in front of the fire department's headquarters in Newton Center, Massachusetts. Chief Randlett, probably the person sitting on the right, bought the car with his own funds.

Two steam-powered 1907 Whites were used in Baltimore. The car on the left carries Chief Engineer George W. Norton, and the car on the right carries Deputy Chief Engineer August Emrich.

Mitchell automobiles were built in Racine, Wisconsin. Milwaukee bought this 1908 Mitchell (right) for use by a chief. To the left is a horse-drawn chemical car.

This 1908 "Carter Two Engine Car" came with two engines that could be operated separately or together. Lettering on the side of the seat says: "CHIEF ENGINEER D.C. FIRE DEPT."

Springfield, Massachusetts, bought this 1908 Knox touring car for its assistant chief. Wording on the hood says: "1st Asst. Engineer S.F.D." A fire extinguisher and Dietz lantern are on the left, and an acetylene floodlight is on dash. Knox autos were built in Springfield.

Chief T. O. Donnell of the St. Louis Salvage Corps is shown at the wheel of this 1908 Overland, which has a fire extinguisher on the running board.

Oldsmobile autos were—and are—manufactured in Lansing, Michigan. The Lansing department used this 1908 Olds to carry its chief.

The first chief's car in San Jose, California, was this 1908 Rambler. In 1910, San Jose's chief was killed when this auto was involved in a wreck.

American-LaFrance, the nation's premier apparatus builder for much of the 20th century, also built a few autos. This 1909 American-LaFrance roadster was a prototype chief's car, carrying a Babcock extinguisher on the running board. To left is a Dietz lantern, and behind the dash is an acetylene floodlight. According to fire apparatus historian John M. Peckham, no records exist that indicate any of these cars actually ended up in fire department service.

Fire Chief's Auto, Rose City Festival Portland,

Bedecked with flowers for the Rose City Parade was this 1909 Pierce-Arrow, the fire chief's car in Portland, Oregon.

A circa-1909 open Cadillac (right) was used in San Diego. The interesting piece of apparatus to the left is a 1910 Seagrave tractor pulling a 75-foot aerial ladder.

Seagrave took over portions of the Frayer-Miller auto firm around 1910. It converted some unsold Frayer-Miller autos to assemble this type of chief's car, which has an ax mounted below the door.

Indianapolis used this 1910 Stoddard-Dayton. The identification "CHIEF I.F.D." is on rear door. Chains, believed to help with traction on dirt roads, are on all four tires. (Note that there is no snow on the ground.)

A 1910 Winton roadster with a chemical tank at the rear, used by an assistant chief in San Jose.

Middletown, New York's chief rode in this 1911 Buick. Wording on hood says: "CHIEF M.F.D."

A circa-1911 Stanley Steamer purchased by the fire chief of Newton Center, Massachusetts. It carries a fire extinguisher on the running board and a Dietz lantern hangs next to the driver. There is a small bell on top of the hood.

A chemical tank and hose basket are at the rear of this 1911 Stoddard-Dayton roadster, used by the chief in Ogden, Utah. Headlights are acetylene and cowl lamps are kerosene. This was Chief A. B. Canefield's auto; later he would be chief at Pocatello, Idaho.

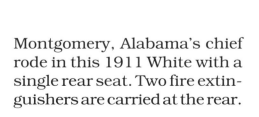

Montgomery, Alabama's chief rode in this 1911 White with a single rear seat. Two fire extinguishers are carried at the rear.

On the left is a 1912 White chief's car, which was built by adding a chemical tank and hose reel to a 3/4-ton chassis. The word "CHIEF" is on the side of the seat. At right is a full-size White chemical and hose car. Both belong to the Charleston, South Carolina, Fire Department.

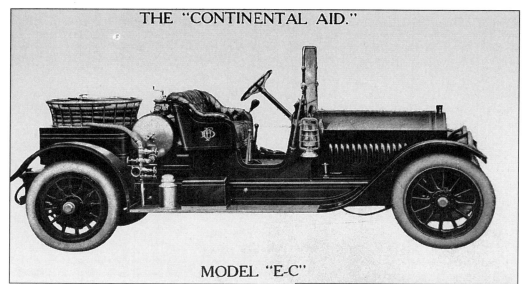

THE "CONTINENTAL AID."

MODEL "E-C"

Ahrens-Fox was a distinguished builder of fire apparatus. In 1913 they offered this model E-C with a chemical tank and referred to it as the "Continental Aid." Cincinnati, Ohio.

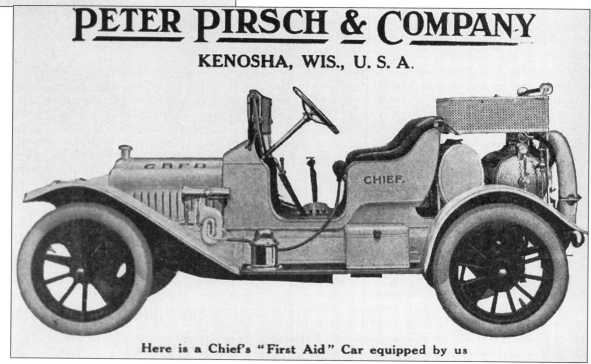

PETER PIRSCH & COMPANY

KENOSHA, WIS., U.S.A.

CHIEF.

Here is a Chief's "First Aid" Car equipped by us

Peter Pirsch & Co., a well-known fire apparatus manufacturer, used a 1913 White chassis to carry a chief's "first aid" rig. Note the chemical tank, hose basket, and spare tire. Cincinnati, Ohio.

The first motorized chief's car in Memphis was this 1914 Cadillac. On the running board are two fire extinguishers and on the other side is a floodlight.

Oakland, California, used this 1914 Cadillac as a chief's car. Later it was converted to a tractor for pulling a city service (ladder) trailer. Note the small bell.

Boise, Idaho, used this 1914 Buick roadster equipped with a chemical tank and hose basket. Chief Fred Windsay is at left, and the driver is J. Boyakin.

The fire chief in Rockland, Massachusetts, provided this 1914 Buick roadster for use as his chief's car.

A 1916 Buick roadster used by Battalion 2's chief in Baltimore. Note the fire extinguisher on the running board.

Parked in front of Station 6 is Oakland, California's 1915 Lozier roadster. The letters "O F D" are on the side. A 1921 American LaFrance is parked in the station.

Detroit, Michigan, used this 1919 Columbia roadster as a chief's car. A bell is mounted in front of the windshield.

A doctor in Vallejo, California, donated this 1919 Dodge to the local fire department. It has both a siren and red light.

This photo was taken in Watsonville, California, in the 1920s and shows both a chief's car and a 1915 Seagrave pumper getting gasoline. Lettering on the side of the car says: "W.F.D. CHIEF."

An early 1920s Cadillac roadster used in Pocatello, Idaho, by the chief of Union Pacific's industrial fire department. It carries a chemical tank in the rear, and the siren is behind the front fender. This photo was taken in 1926.

This four-passenger 1926 Buick coupe was a chief's car in Milwaukee, Wisconsin. Damage to its side indicates it has been in an accident. There is snow on the ground and the car has chains on its rear wheels.

The chief of Philadelphia's Battalion 9 rode in this 1926 Lincoln. A red light and bell are mounted in front. Rope for a bell can be seen along the side of this right-side door.

A mid-1920s Ford that was once used in Roanoke County, Virginia. It has both a siren and red light.

In large cities, insurance companies funded salvage corps. These salvage corps responded to fires in apparatus carrying tarpaulins and other gear that could reduce the damage to a building's contents caused by smoke and water. In Baltimore, the chief of the salvage corps used this 1927 Marmon. A locomotive bell is carried in front.

This circa-1928 Chevrolet was originally the chief's car in Roseville, California. It later became a clown's car. Note that the hub on the rear wheel is off-center, which would yield a unique ride. Headlights are not original.

A 1928 Studebaker brougham, used in Tacoma, Washington, has the letters "T F D" on door. The siren is behind the bumper.

A 1929 Cadillac roadster used by Battalion 8's chief in Philadelphia. The cord from the bell clapper stretches back inside the cab. The siren is above the bumper.

This 1931 Ford A roadster was used as a chief's car by the volunteer department in Sandy Springs, Maryland. A small red light is in front of the radiator and sealed-beam headlights have been installed.

One of the few 1930s convertibles used to carry a chief is this 1934 Graham Bluestreak, used in Pocatello, Idaho. The siren and red lights are between the bumper and grille.

A 1935 Chrysler Airflow four-door sedan was used as the chief's car in Memphis. A Mars oscillating red light is mounted above the siren in front. The car has two radio antennae.

This 1935 Ford was used by the Chicago Fire Department. One headlight lens is red, the other green. The top of the car is painted black, similar to the paint scheme used on Chicago apparatus. The rack in front of the bumper carries a Mars light and bell. A single windshield wiper is on the driver's side, and a spotlight is on the passenger's side.

Two views of a 1936 Buick four-door used by the fire chief in Baltimore, Maryland. A bell is carried on the passenger's side, and a cable for ringing the bell can be seen leading downward to the running board. The siren is in front and the red light is on the driver's side.

The Battalion chief in charge of the Baltimore Fire Department's Marine Division used this 1937 Chevrolet coupe.

A four-door 1937 Buick used in Kansas City, Missouri. The siren and light are above the bumper. The car is painted two colors. On the left is a 1927 Ahrens-Fox pumper.

The chief of Battalion 1 in Baltimore rode in this 1938 Buick coupe, which has a bell, siren, and red light.

The chief of the Underwriters Patrol in Kansas City, Kansas, used this 1940 Packard four-door sedan. A Federal double-tone siren and red light are mounted in front.

This 1941 DeSoto four-door was used by the assistant chief in South San Francisco, California. Red lights are carried above the front bumper and the car has two radio antennae.

A common setting for a chief's car was in an assembled "portrait" of a department's fleet. On the right is a 1942 Nash, a battalion chief's car in the Milwaukee Fire Department. Behind it are an REO fuel tanker, Pirsch pumper, Mack pumper, FWD wrecker, Pirsch aerial, and a service truck.

Wesley Powell, Battalion 4's Chief in the Los Angeles County Fire Department, stands in front of his 1947 Ford.

Reading, Pennsylvania, used this 1947 Chrysler coupe for its chief's car. The car carries an oscillating red light on the roof, a red light/siren combination on each front fender, and a bell in front.

A 1946-48 DeSoto used in New York City. It has red lights on both fenders, an oscillating light on the roof, and bell in front.

The chief's car in Norfolk, Virginia, was this 1947 Hudson four-door. It has a roof-mounted warning light and double-tone coaster siren.

This 1948 Ford two-door was used by the fire chief in Iron Mountain, Michigan. Two red lights are mounted on the front bumper, and a radio antenna is in the rear.

A 1949 Frazer Vagabond used as the chief's car in Clifton, New Jersey. The Vagabond's trunk and rear window opened and the rear seat folded forward so a stretcher could be carried.

A 1950 Buick Special used by a district chief in Baltimore.

A 1951 Ford club coupe used by Battalion 14's chief in Chicago. A siren and oscillating red light are on the roof, and red lights are on each front fender. The car is red, with a black top,

The marshal of the 3rd Division in Chicago's Fire Department rode in this 1953 Buick Special.

The chief of the Central Fire Protection District 4 in Santa Clara County, California, used this 1953 Ford F-250 pickup. It carries a fire extinguisher and a "slip-in" pump, hose, and water tank unit in the truck bed.

A deputy chief in Baltimore used this 1955 Ford station wagon.

Chicago rebuilt a 1955 Flxible city bus for use as a fire department communications and command center.

A 1960 Chevrolet Corvair used in Portland, Maine, to promote fire prevention. Note the head of Sparky, with helmet, on the roof.

A fire prevention battalion chief in Baltimore rode in this 1960 Ford four-door station wagon.

This 1961 Ford station wagon was a battalion chief's car in San Jose, California. A record of the equipment it carried was found in the rear: 5 pounds of CO_2, three masks, an oxygen bottle, a saw, a cutting torch, fuse, hose bridges, smoke ejector (fan), battery jumper cable, sprinkler head shutoff tools, high-voltage tools and gloves, asbestos blanket, 150 feet of electrical cord, electric adapters, and 100 feet of 1/2-inch rope.

This 1962 Ford F-2 pickup was used by a battalion chief in the Santa Clara County (California) Fire Protection District.

This 1964 Chevrolet was used in Mountain View, California.

A battalion chief in the Santa Clara County (California) Fire Protection District rode in this 1964 International station wagon. Note the air horn on the front fender.

A 1967 GMC used as a communications van by the San Francisco Fire Department.

The chief of the San Mateo-Santa Cruz Ranger Unit in the California Department of Forestry used this 1968 Kaiser Jeep. The top is enclosed.

A 1968 Plymouth station wagon used in Baltimore.

Seattle used this large 1970 Chevrolet van as a command car.

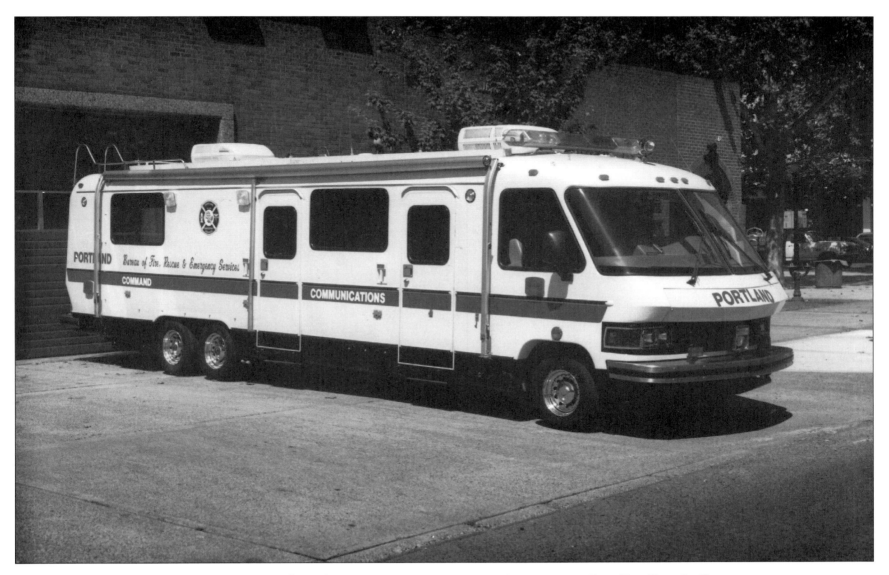

Revcon built of this 1970 command and communications van. It was used in Portland, Oregon.

California's Division of Forestry used this 1971 International with a school bus body for a communications unit. It was stationed at Morgan Hill, California.

This 1972 Nash Matador was painted lime green and was used by a district chief in San Jose, California.

Ketchum, Idaho, used this 1972 Clark Cortez for a mobile command unit.

Philadelphia used this 1974 International chassis to carry a communications van body.

Boise, Idaho, used this 1974 Chevrolet can. The words "COMMAND OFFICER" are on the side.

The chief in Gilroy, California, used this 1974 Chevrolet El Camino.

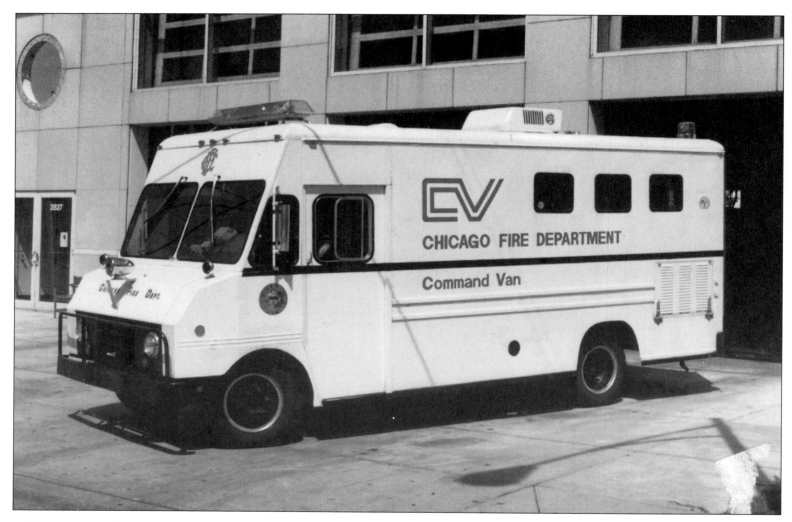

A Boyertown body on a 1975 Ford was used for this command van in Chicago.

Battalion 2's chief in Baltimore used this 1976 Ford station wagon, painted orange with a white top.

The Baltimore Fire Department chief used this 1976 Dodge. It is properly parked in front of the sign saying: "PARKING RESERVED FOR CHIEF, FIRE DEPT."

In Zayante, California, this 1978 Jeep served as the chief's car. Note the fire rake and shovel on the roof.

A circa-1980 Jeep used by the California Division of Forestry station in Ukiah, California.

An early 1980s American Eagle wagon with all-wheel drive used by the fire protection district in Tahoe City, California, an area known for deep snows.

Battalion 5's chief in San Francisco used this 1982 Chevrolet Malibu four-door sedan. Note the special wheels.

A 1983 Dodge Ramcharger used in Fairfield, California.

A San Francisco battalion chief used this 1983 Chevrolet Blazer.

The fire department in Santa Clara, California, used this 1984 Grumman Kurbmaster on a Chevrolet chassis for a hazardous materials incident command car.

A long-wheelbase 1985 Ford with a super cab used by the California Division of Forestry in Napa.

A deputy chief in Seattle used this 1985 GMC suburban with four-wheel drive.

This 1986 Plymouth four-door was a chief's car in Seattle.

Seattle District 10's chief utilized this 1987 Chevrolet four-door.

A battalion chief in Portland, Oregon, used this 1987 Dodge. Behind the rear seat is a mesh net to keep material in the rear from coming forward in case of a sudden stop.

Scotts Valley, California's chief rode in the 1987 Dodge Ram Charger.

This 1987 Dodge four-door was the chief's car in Santa Clara, California.

This 1988 Jeep Cherokee was the chief's car in Aromas, California.

Battalion 4's chief in Phoenix rode in this 1989 Chevrolet suburban wagon.

In Phoenix, Arizona, the chief of Battalion 10 uses this 1990 Chevrolet suburban. Note the extra lights mounted on the bumper.

Tacoma, Washington's Battalion 2 chief uses this 1990 Chevrolet van. It has light bars both front and rear, and an illuminating light facing this side.

A 1990 Jeep Cherokee served as the chief's car in Elko, Nevada.

San Francisco uses this 1991 Ford panel truck as an incident command unit. It is equipped with a wooden desk console and cabinets. Note the reverse lettering on the hood.

A 1992 Plymouth Voyager used by the Battalion 6 chief in Seattle. The siren is in front of the grille, and a light bar is on the roof.

A battalion chief in Palo Alto, California, rides in this 1992 GMC. It has a light bar and spotlight on the roof.

Battalion 1's deputy chief of operations in Seattle used this 1993 GMC all-wheel-drive suburban.

Seattle used this 1993 Peterbilt with a Mobile Tech body as an incident command unit.

Battalion 2's chief in the Santa Clara County (California) Fire Protection District rides in this 1994 Chevrolet suburban. It has push bars in front and a light bar on the roof.

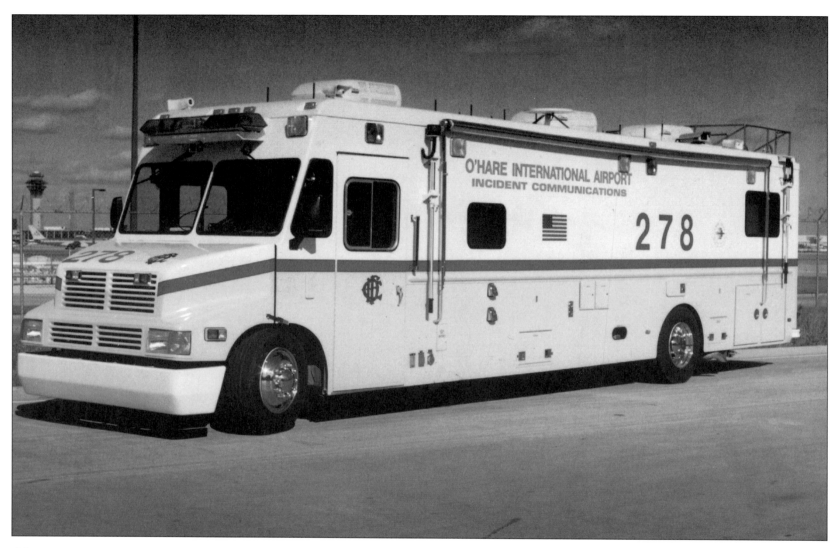

Chicago's O'Hare Airport uses this 1994 International for its mobile incident command post.

In San Jose, California, Battalion 13's chief rides in this 1995 Chevrolet suburban.

The chief of the fire protection district in Carmel, California, rides in this 1996 Ford LTD Crown Victoria. On the front bumper, the word "FIRE" is painted in reverse so it can be seen correctly in one's rearview mirror, although the placement of the lettering seems low.

This 1997 Spartan 3D used in Santa Clara, California combines three functions. It is a command center, a heavy rescue, and a hazardous materials truck. The area behind the cab holds desks and computers.

Index by Automakers

CREDITS:

PAGE 4: San Francisco Fire Department
PAGE 7: Seagrave
PAGE 8: Wayne Sorensen Collection
PAGE 9 (top): New York City Fire Department,**(bottom):** Wayne Sorensen Collection
PAGE 10 (top): Wayne Sorensen Collection **(bottom):** San Francisco Fire Department
PAGE 11: Waterous
PAGE 12: Newton Center Fire Department
PAGE 13: Bill Snyder
PAGE 14: Wayne Sorensen Collection
PAGE 15 (top): Wayne Sorensen Collection, **(bottom):** Knox Motor Company
PAGE 16: Bill Snyder
PAGE 17 (top): Wayne Sorensen Collection, **(bottom):** San Jose Fire Department
PAGE 18: American LaFrance
PAGE 19: Portland Fire Department
PAGE 20: Walt Pittman Collection
PAGE 21: Seagrave
PAGE 22 (top): Indianapolis Fire Department, **(bottom):** San Jose Fire Department
PAGE 23 (top): Middletown Fire Department, **(bottom):** Newton Center Fire Department
PAGE 24 (top): Oakland Fire Department, **(bottom):** Montgomery Fire Department
PAGE 25: Charleston Fire Department
PAGE 26 (top): Ahrens Fox, **(bottom):** Peter Pirsch Company
PAGE 27 (Top): Memphis Fire Department, **(bottom):** Oakland Fire Department
PAGE 28 (top): Boise Fire Department, **(bottom):** Wayne Sorensen Collection
PAGE 29 (top): Bill Snyder, **(bottom):** Oakland Fire Department
PAGE 30 (top): Detroit Fire Department, **(bottom):** Wayne Sorensen Collection
PAGE 31: Watsonville Fire Department
PAGE 32: O.S.L. Railroad

PAGE 33: Milwaukee Fire Department
PAGE 34: Philadelphia Fire Department
PAGE 35: Bill Snyder
PAGE 36: Bill Snyder
PAGE 37: Paul Darrell
PAGE 38: Ralph Decker
PAGE 39: Philadelphia, PA
PAGE 40: Bill Snyder
PAGE 41: Pocatello Fire Department
PAGE 42: Memphis Fire Department
PAGE 43: Roland Boulet
PAGE 44 (both): Bill Snyder
PAGE 45: Bill Snyder
PAGE 46: Kansas City Fire Department
PAGE 47: Bill Snyder
PAGE 48: Bill Snyder
PAGE 49: Dale Magee
PAGE 50: Milwaukee Fire Department
PAGE 51: Dale Magee
PAGE 52: Bill Snyder
PAGE 53: Bill Snyder
PAGE 54: Wayne Sorensen Collection
PAGE 55: Wayne Sorensen Collection
PAGE 56: Kaizer-Frazer Corp.
PAGE 57: Bill Snyder
PAGE 58: Bob Freeman
PAGE 59: Bob Freeman
PAGE 60: Central Fire District Santa Clara County, CA
PAGE 61: Bill Snyder
PAGE 62: Bill Friedrich
PAGE 63: Wayne Sorensen Collection
PAGE 64 (top): Wayne Sorensen Collection, **(bottom):** Bill Snyder
PAGE 65: Central Fire District Santa Clara County, CA
PAGE 66 (both): Wayne Sorensen Collection
PAGE 67: San Francisco Fire Department
PAGE 68: Wayne Sorensen Collection
PAGE 69: Bill Snyder

PAGE 70: Bill Hattersley
PAGE 71: Bill Hattersley
PAGE 72: Wayne Sorensen Collection
PAGE 73: Wayne Sorensen Collection
PAGE 74: Bill Hattersley
PAGE 75: Bill Friedrich
PAGE 76: Wayne Sorensen Collection
PAGE 77: Wayne Sorensen Collection
PAGE 78: Bill Hattersley
PAGE 79: Bill Snyder
PAGE 80: Bill Snyder
PAGE 81: Wayne Sorensen Collection
PAGE 82: Wayne Sorensen Collection
PAGE 83: Wayne Sorensen Collection
PAGE 84: Bill Hattersley
PAGE 85: Wayne Sorensen Collection
PAGE 86: Wayne Sorensen Collection
PAGE 87: Wayne Sorensen Collection
PAGE 88: Wayne Sorensen Collection
PAGE 89: Bill Hattersley
PAGE 90: Bill Hattersley
PAGE 91: Bill Hattersley
PAGE 92: Bill Hattersley
PAGE 93: Wayne Sorensen Collection
PAGE 94: Wayne Sorensen Collection
PAGE 95: Wayne Sorensen Collection
PAGE 96: Bill Hattersley
PAGE 97: Bill Hattersley
PAGE 98: Bill Hattersley
PAGE 99: Wayne Sorensen Collection
PAGE 100: Wayne Sorensen Collection
PAGE 101: Bill Hattersley
PAGE 102: Wayne Sorensen Collection
PAGE 103: Bill Hattersley
PAGE 104: Bill Hattersley
PAGE 105: Wayne Sorensen Collection
PAGE 106: Bill Friedrich
PAGE 107: Wayne Sorensen Collection
PAGE 108: (both): Wayne Sorensen Collection

The Iconografix Photo Archive Series includes:

AMERICAN CULTURE
AMERICAN SERVICE STATIONS 1935-1943   ISBN 1-882256-27-1
COCA-COLA: A HISTORY IN PHOTOGRAPHS
    1930-1969   ISBN 1-882256-46-8
COCA-COLA: ITS VEHICLES IN PHOTOGRAPHS
    1930-1969   ISBN 1-882256-47-6
PHILLIPS 66 1945-1954   ISBN 1-882256-42-5

AUTOMOTIVE
FERRARI PININFARINA 1952-1996   ISBN 1-882256-65-4
GT40   ISBN 1-882256-64-6
IMPERIAL 1955-1963   ISBN 1-882256-22-0
IMPERIAL 1964-1968   ISBN 1-882256-23-9
LE MANS 1950: THE BRIGGS CUNNINGHAM
    CAMPAIGN   ISBN 1-882256-21-2
LINCOLN MOTOR CARS 1920-1942   ISBN 1-882256-57-3
LINCOLN MOTOR CARS 1946-1960   ISBN 1-882256-58-1
MG 1945-1964   ISBN 1-882256-52-2
MG 1965-1980   ISBN 1-882256-53-0
PACKARD MOTOR CARS 1935-1942   ISBN 1-882256-44-1
PACKARD MOTOR CARS 1946-1958   ISBN 1-882256-45-X
SEBRING 12-HOUR RACE 1970   ISBN 1-882256-20-4
STUDEBAKER 1933-1942   ISBN 1-882256-24-7
STUDEBAKER 1946-1958   ISBN 1-882256-25-5
VANDERBILT CUP RACE 1936 & 1937   ISBN 1-882256-66-2

TRACTORS AND CONSTRUCTION EQUIPMENT
CASE TRACTORS 1912-1959   ISBN 1-882256-32-8
CATERPILLAR MILITARY TRACTORS
    VOLUME 1   ISBN 1-882256-16-6
CATERPILLAR MILITARY TRACTORS
    VOLUME 2   ISBN 1-882256-17-4
CATERPILLAR SIXTY   ISBN 1-882256-05-0
CLETRAC AND OLIVER CRAWLERS   ISBN 1-882256-43-3
ERIE SHOVEL   ISBN 1-882256-69-7
FARMALL CUB   ISBN 1-882256-71-9
FARMALL F–SERIES   ISBN 1-882256-02-6
FARMALL MODEL H   ISBN 1-882256-03-4
FARMALL MODEL M   ISBN 1-882256-15-8
FARMALL REGULAR   ISBN 1-882256-14-X
FARMALL SUPER SERIES   ISBN 1-882256-49-2
FORDSON 1917-1928   ISBN 1-882256-33-6
HART-PARR   ISBN 1-882256-08-5
HOLT TRACTORS   ISBN 1-882256-10-7
INTERNATIONAL TRACTRACTOR   ISBN 1-882256-48-4
INTERNATIONAL TD CRAWLERS 1933-1962   ISBN 1-882256-72-7
JOHN DEERE MODEL A   ISBN 1-882256-12-3
JOHN DEERE MODEL B   ISBN 1-882256-01-8
JOHN DEERE MODEL D   ISBN 1-882256-00-X
JOHN DEERE 30 SERIES   ISBN 1-882256-13-1
MINNEAPOLIS-MOLINE U-SERIES   ISBN 1-882256-07-7
OLIVER TRACTORS   ISBN 1-882256-09-3

RUSSELL GRADERS   ISBN 1-882256-11-5
TWIN CITY TRACTOR   ISBN 1-882256-06-9

RAILWAYS
CHICAGO, ST. PAUL, MINNEAPOLIS & OMAHA
    RAILWAY 1880-1940   ISBN 1-882256-67-0
CHICAGO&NORTH WESTERN RAILWAY 1975-1995   ISBN 1-882256-76-X
GREAT NORTHERN RAILWAY 1945-1970   ISBN 1-882256-56-5
GREAT NORTHERN RAILWAY 1945-1970 VOLUME 2   ISBN 1-882256-79-4
MILWAUKEE ROAD 1850-1960   ISBN 1-882256-61-1
SOO LINE 1975-1992   ISBN 1-882256-68-9
WISCONSIN CENTRAL LIMITED 1987-1996   ISBN 1-882256-75-1
WISCONSIN CENTRAL RAILWAY 1871-1909   ISBN 1-882256-78-6

TRUCKS
AMERICAN LaFRANCE 700 SERIES 1945-1952   ISBN 1-882256-90-5
BEVERAGE TRUCKS 1910-1975   ISBN 1-882256-60-3
BROCKWAY TRUCKS 1948-1961*   ISBN 1-882256-55-7
DODGE TRUCKS 1929-1947   ISBN 1-882256-36-0
DODGE TRUCKS 1948-1960   ISBN 1-882256-37-9
DODGE POWER WAGONS 1940-1980   ISBN 1-882256-89-1
LOGGING TRUCKS 1915-1970   ISBN 1-882256-59-X
MACK® MODEL AB*   ISBN 1-882256-18-2
MACK AP SUPER-DUTY TRUCKS 1926-1938*   ISBN 1-882256-54-9
MACK MODEL B 1953-1966 VOLUME 1*   ISBN 1-882256-19-0
MACK MODEL B 1953-1966 VOLUME 2*   ISBN 1-882256-34-4
MACK EB-EC-ED-EE-EF-EG-DE 1936-1951*   ISBN 1-882256-29-8
MACK EH-EJ-EM-EQ-ER-ES 1936-1950*   ISBN 1-882256-39-5
MACK FC-FCSW-NW 1936-1947*   ISBN 1-882256-28-X
MACK FG-FH-FJ-FK-FN-FP-FT-FW 1937-1950*   ISBN 1-882256-35-2
MACK LF-LH-LJ-LM-LT 1940-1956 *   ISBN 1-882256-38-7
MACK MODEL B FIRE TRUCKS 1954-1966*   ISBN 1-882256-62-X
MACK MODEL CF FIRE TRUCKS 1967-1981*   ISBN 1-882256-63-8
MACK MODEL L FIRE TRUCKS 1940-1954*   ISBN 1-882256-86-7
STUDEBAKER TRUCKS 1927-1940   ISBN 1-882256-40-9
STUDEBAKER TRUCKS 1941-1964   ISBN 1-882256-41-7
WHITE TRUCKS 1900-1937   ISBN 1-882256-80-8

* This product is sold under license from Mack Trucks, Inc. All rights reserved.

The Iconografix Photo Gallery Series includes:
CATERPILLAR PHOTO GALLERY   ISBN 1-882256-70-0
MACK TRUCKS PHOTO GALLERY   ISBN 1-882256-88-3

The Iconografix Photo Album Series includes:
CADILLAC 1948-1964   ISBN 1-882256-83-2
CORVETTE PROTOTYPES & SHOW CARS   ISBN 1-882256-77-8
DODGE PICKUPS 1939-1978   ISBN 1-882256-82-4
FIRE CHIEF CARS 1900-1997   ISBN 1-882256-87-5
LOLA RACE CARS 1962-1990   ISBN 1-882256-73-5
LOTUS RACE CARS 1961-1994   ISBN 1-882256-84-0
McLAREN RACE CARS 1965-1996   ISBN 1-882256-74-3
PORSCHE 356 1948-1965   ISBN 1-882256-85-9

All Iconografix books are available from direct mail specialty book dealers and bookstores worldwide, or can be ordered from the publisher. For book trade and distribution information or to add your name to our mailing list contact

Iconografix
PO Box 446
Hudson, Wisconsin, 54016

Telephone: (715) 381-9755
(800) 289-3504 (USA)
Fax: (715) 381-9756

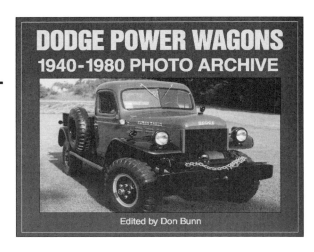
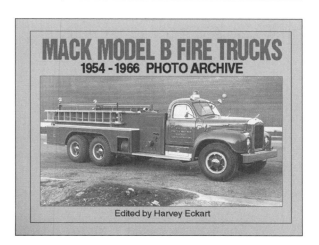

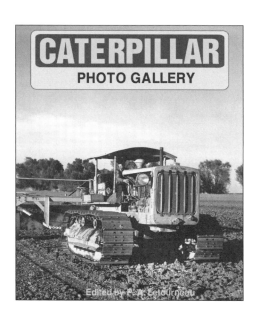
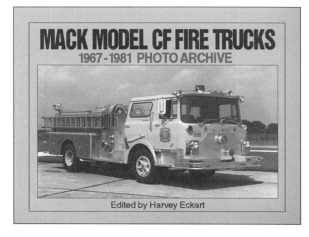